12-25-96

Jesus
Son of
Mary

Jesus Son of Mary

A LIGUORI CLASSIC

Fulton J. Sheen

Illustrated by Grady Gunter

LIGUORI
PUBLICATIONS

One Liguori Drive
Liguori, MO 63057-9999
(314) 464-2500

ISBN 0-89243-783-9

Library of Congress Catalog Card Number: 94-73022

Original edition copyright © 1947 by The Declan X. McMullen Company, Inc.

This edition copyright © 1995 by Liguori Publications.

Printed in the United States of America.

95 96 97 98 99   5 4 3 2 1

Dedicated to the

Virgin Mother

of the Infant Son of God

in token of love and gratitude

His Birth

YOU KNOW there is a God in Heaven. But did you ever think about Him coming to this earth? And what shape He would take when He decided to come here to help us?

Would He come as a cloud in the sky…a flash of lightning…a peal of thunder?

God really did come to this earth. That is the meaning of Christmas—God with us.

But He did not come as anything strange or frightening or huge.

He came as a Baby to a tiny little village called Bethlehem.

And He was called Jesus.

You would not like to take your soul, which can know and think and love and talk, and put it into the body of a snake or a cat or a dog, would you?

But God did more than that when He became man.

He stepped down from Heaven and became like one of us.

It was not even like the smartest boy in the eighth grade going to the bottom of the class in the first grade.

And He did not come to us as a great man but as a very simple Baby.

YOU NEVER KNEW where or when or how you would be born. But Jesus did. And that is because He is God.

Nobody knew fifty years ago that you would be born. But for hundreds of years many people knew that Jesus would be born of a Mother who would be a virgin.

8

They knew also the time and the very town where He would first appear.

He who later on called Himself "the Living Bread descended from Heaven" was born in Bethlehem—which in Hebrew means "house of bread." And He was laid in a manger—a place of food—as if to show us that as we have bread for our bodies, so He would be the Bread for our souls.

IN THIS WORLD, people who are proud and who think they are terribly important cannot get used to the idea of God making Himself so little.

That is why only two kinds of people came to visit Him when He was born—the Shepherds and the Wise Men.

The Shepherds were very simple people. They were sure that they did not know anything. The Wise Men were very wise. But they knew that they did not know everything.

People who think that they know everything never find that Baby.

Angel choirs sang to the Shepherds, saying: "Your Shepherd is born in Bethlehem."

A giant star appeared, bigger than all the stars of heaven, to lead the Wise Men.

They followed it until it stopped over a stable.

They went in with the Shepherds and found the Baby Jesus in a manger with His Mother and Joseph.

There was an ox on one side of Him and a donkey on the other to help keep Him warm.

Wouldn't you think that when God came to this earth, He could find a

better home than a stable?

Well, His Mother tried to find one.

She went to all the hotels in the village of Bethlehem.

But there was always the same answer: "There is no room."

THE THREE WISE MEN brought gifts to the Baby.

One brought gold, because He is the King of the world, and kings usually wear golden ornaments.

Another brought incense, because He is God and ought to be surrounded with sweet-smelling odors as He is adored.

Another brought myrrh—a kind of medicine used to soften wounds.

The Wise Man who brought the myrrh knew that evil men would not like anyone as good as Jesus, and one day they would kill Him.

Think of how sad your own mother would have been if someone brought her myrrh when you were born.

Well, His Mother was very sad, for a cruel death was in store for her divine little Son. As she stood at the stable door one sunset and stretched out her arms wide, she saw the shadow of a cross fall on the crib of her little Boy.

His Boyhood

YOU HAVE HEARD many stories of kings.

The king who lived in the land where Jesus was born was very wicked.
When he heard Jesus was a heavenly King, he was afraid he would lose

the land he ruled over.

How foolish he was!

He forgot that Jesus, who gave up His heavenly crown, would certainly not want to steal an earthly one.

Jesus did not want the kind of a kingdom that soldiers had to keep together. He wanted a Kingdom of all people, who would love Him and always do what He asked.

This evil king was very jealous of Jesus. He sent out his horsemen to break into houses and to stab to death all the little boys in and around Bethlehem.

He thought that, if he killed all the new baby boys, he would be sure to kill the Baby Jesus.

The little children who died that day are called the Holy Innocents.

They were like ships that sank just after they first put out to sea. They died for the Lord before He died for them.

BUT THE SOLDIERS never found Jesus.

An angel came in the night and told Joseph to take Mary and the Child into far-off Egypt.

There is an old legend which says that, when Jesus came into Egypt, many statues of false gods toppled over and crashed to the ground.

But, what is certain is that a prophet who lived long before Jesus came foretold that Jesus the true God would be a refugee in Egypt—as His own people were fourteen hundred years before.

Every missionary who ever goes into a pagan land finds strength to do it because Jesus did it first.

When the evil king died, the angel came again and told Joseph: "Now you may go back to your own land."

So Joseph returned to his own village, called Nazareth, and reopened his little shop.

He was a carpenter.

And the Boy Jesus watched him and learned how to use a hammer and saw. He worked as a carpenter because He wanted to show how much God loves work.

He who made the stars and the sun and the moon let Joseph tell Him how to make a chair and a table and a door.

His Mother was often worried when she saw Him with nails in His hands, and she was always afraid that one lying on the floor might pierce His feet.

WHEN HE WAS TWELVE, like many other boys, He got lost. But unlike other boys, He got lost on purpose.

He had gone with Mary and Joseph and lots of others to the largest city in His country to pray.

When the services were over, His Mother and Joseph started back, His Mother traveling with the women, and Joseph with the men. Each thought that Jesus was safely with the other group.

When they discovered that He was missing, they were very frightened.

They searched for three days before they found Him.

And where do you think He had been?

Because He was God and knew all that would happen to Him, I think that one night He went to visit an olive garden where, many years later, He would go to pray for the world.

On another night, perhaps, He walked outside of the city to a hill which was called Calvary.

Calvary—remember that name, you will hear it again!

Anyhow they found Him on the third day. He was teaching the wisest men of the city—although He was only a Boy.

He could do that because He was God.

Then He went back with His parents to Nazareth and obeyed them until He was thirty years old.

He did this to show how much He wants us to obey His commandment: Honor thy father and thy mother! And also to remind us that it takes a good family to produce good children.

God does not want parents to quarrel and leave each other and their children. His own family was happy because it takes more than two to make love.

The Third in the family at Nazareth was Jesus.

His Mother

YOU DID NOT MAKE your own mother. You could not!

But if you could, you certainly would have made her what you think she is now—the nicest mother in all the world.

But Jesus could make His own Mother because He is God. He lived in Heaven long before His Mother was born.

Don't you think, therefore, that He would make her the purest, the loveliest, and the most beautiful Mother who ever lived?

She was so good that He decided He did not want to keep her just for Himself!

That would be selfish—even for God.

Jesus wanted her to be the Mother of everyone in the world.

She was good enough to be that because she was always looking out for the needs of everyone else.

We see that in what happened at a party in Cana.

WHEN JESUS WAS THIRTY years old, He and His Mother were invited to a wedding feast.

In that country people drank wine with their meals.

But at this party, before the dinner was over, they found that there was not going to be enough wine to go around.

Mary noticed this first.

She went to her Son and said: "They have no wine."

She knew He could do wonderful things, because He was God. And Jesus would not refuse anything His dear Mother wanted.

There were six large pots nearby. Jesus told the waiters to fill them with water.

Then He told them to taste what was in the pots.

They were surprised to find that the water had become wine!

And when they served it at the table, it was so good that the guests asked: "Why did you keep the best wine until now?"

Jesus always remembered how much His Mother loved others, as if she wanted to be everyone else's Mother too.

He also knew how much she wanted others to obey Him because that day she said to the waiters: "Do what He tells you."

Three years later when Jesus was dying, He gave away His Mother!

He could do that too, because He was God. Turning to one of His dearest friends, John, and making him stand for everyone in the world, Jesus said: "Behold thy Mother."

And from that day to this, each of us has two mothers.

Our own mother who gave us flesh and blood and Mary who gave us Jesus.

Don't forget her!

You would not like it if someone came into your house and never said a word to your mother or pretended that she did not exist.

Well, do you think that Jesus would like us if we did not love His Mother? Or if we did not pray to her?

Learn then, by heart, that lovely prayer, the *Hail Mary*.

His Stories

OUR LORD CALLED Himself the Good Shepherd.

By this He meant that we are His sheep, and that He watches over us and cares for us and knows each one of us by name.

We are not just a part of a crowd because each of us has a soul.

He gave us that soul when He first made us. It is worth more than anything else in the world.

When a soul is lost by sin, as a lamb may be lost among the thorns, He leaves the flock that is safe and seeks to find the lamb that is lost. When He finds it, He puts it on His shoulders and brings it back to the house to rest and get well.

To be happy we must follow Jesus and love Him, as sheep follow a shepherd and do his bidding.

JESUS TOLD stories better than anyone, and every story tells us how we ought to live.

He warned us never to brag.

God refused to hear the prayer of a man who went boldly to the front of the church and boasted to God of all the good things he did. He was asking to be praised; and God did not like the way he acted.

But another man, who was not proud, stayed at the back of the temple. This man spoke to God of the bad things he did and asked to be forgiven. God listened willingly to him.

Jesus asked us not to sound a trumpet ever time we do a good deed.
Keep it secret, He said. You will get your real reward in Heaven.

HE WARNED US never to forget to be thankful.

Ten men, who had a disease so foul that they had to live outside of the city gates, once asked Him to cure them.

He did so and they ran off, happy to be well again. Only one of them bothered to come back and thank Him.

Jesus asked: "Where are the other nine?"

How few there are whoever thank God for His favors!

H<small>E</small> **WARNED US** never to judge people by the country they come from or the color of their skin or the amount of money they have. These things come by chance; they are extra.

What is important, Jesus said, is not the outside of the cup, but the inside. It is what is in the heart that counts.

You have heard people say: "If someone hits you, hit him back."

Jesus said: "Don't hit him back."

He meant that if someone does something mean to you, don't try to get back at him. When you do this, you only make hate grow.

People who do mean things are like dry flowers in a desert. They are thirsty and parched. When you show them kindness, it gives them what they need, and they change.

Put love where you do not find it and everyone becomes loveable.

O<small>NE</small> very interesting thing that Jesus said was: "Unless you become as little children, you will not enter the Kingdom of Heaven."

If we believe what God teaches us, we become His children forever.

M<small>ANY</small> of these thoughts Jesus gave to his people in His Sermon on the Mount. But they did not listen to Him.

Three years later they put Him to death on another mount—the Hill of Calvary.

His Crucifixion

A GANG of bad boys throw stones at a good boy when he tells them it is wrong to steal.

That is why evil men wanted to kill Jesus.

There were men who wanted to run the world by telling other people what to do. They did not like Him because He told them that they had to make themselves better first.

So, one night they arrested Him while He was praying in an olive garden.

One of His own friends, Judas, told the gang where He was. They had promised to pay him thirty pieces of silver.

God can be sold so cheaply.

Then a dictator sentenced Him to die on a hill called Calvary—remember?

BUT HOW was He killed?

If you drive a stick into the ground, it points up to Heaven. That stick stands for doing what God asks. If you take another stick and nail it across the first, that stands for what you want to do, not what God wants.

It crosses the other stick—and you have made a cross.

So they nailed Jesus to a cross. He could have turned the nails into roses and the cross into a golden throne if He wanted—because He is God. But He chose to suffer for our sins.

When most men are sent to death, they either blame the judges or say they are innocent or ask to be forgiven.

But Jesus, who had preached "Love your enemies," did something no one had ever done.

He asked that those who pierced His hands and feet be forgiven. He said: "They know not what they do."

Two thieves were set on crosses on the same day—one on either side of Jesus.

The one on the right side was sorry for his sins and asked to be taken up with God.

So Jesus told him: "This day thou shalt be with Me in Heaven."

The other thief cried out to be taken down from the cross.

He wanted only his body saved—not his soul. He didn't think of Heaven at all.

Some people are like that. They forget that God gives us what we need, but not always what we want.

SOME EVIL MEN stood beneath His cross and clenched their fists and shouted: "If you are God, save yourself."

But He did not act as a coward. He was there to help all of us who need help.

The rain cannot save itself if it is to fall over the earth and make the flowers bloom.

A soldier cannot think first of himself if he is to save his country.

And Jesus could not save Himself if He was to save us and pay our debts for our sins.

The very God whose Love we hurt whenever we sin came to free us from sin and make us His friends again.

IF YOU were fishing at a river's bank and someone came up and threw himself into the river and was drowned, just to prove how much he loved you, you would say it was silly and foolish.

But if you had fallen into the river and were drowning and someone jumped in to save you, then you would say: "That person loves me."

And so, whenever you see Jesus on the cross you ought to say:

"Greater love than this no one has—that He lay down His life for His friend!"

THIRTY YEARS He spent obeying; three years in teaching. And now the three hours of saving us were up.

Death did not come to Him; He went to greet it.

He gave up this life willingly. No one took it away.

When He died, the sun hid itself—it was ashamed to shed its light on a wicked world. The earth shook, and the dead came from their graves.

A sergeant in the Roman army, who did not believe in God, ran up to thrust a spear into His side. Then he suddenly realized what he had done. He believed and said: "Indeed, this is the Son of God."

No truer words were ever spoken.

He was taken down from the cross and laid in the arms of His Mother.

She had lost her Son in the battle against evil.

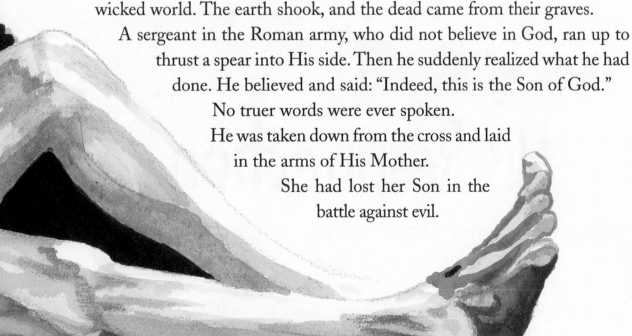

His Resurrection

WHEN THE EVENING of Good Friday came, His body was unfastened from the cross. His friends wrapped it in spices and in myrrh, and laid it in a tomb cut out of solid rock.

Then everyone remembered what Jesus had once said: "After three days I will rise again."

HIS ENEMIES WERE AFRAID that He might really do this. So they went to a judge to get soldiers to guard the tomb. They thought that the Apostles might steal His body and say that He had risen.

One might as well put soldiers guarding an oak tree in winter so that fresh leaves will not grow in the spring.

We've often stamped on a blackened seed. Yet we have seen the flower, in hues as red as a robin's breast, wake from what we thought was dead.

But men were not yet convinced that Jesus, who made all nature, would rise again as He foretold. They rolled a great, heavy stone across His grave and set soldiers to watch it day and night.

On the third day, which we call Easter, an angel from Heaven rolled away the stone and the guards fell down as if dead with fear.

Jesus had risen from the dead!

His face was like the glorious sun and His garments were white as snow.

That morning, three women came to His tomb. And the angel said to them: "He is not here. Go tell Peter and the rest that He is risen."

Peter and John would not believe them at first. But when Jesus came to them with glorious scars still on His body, they recognized Him and were glad.

One of them, Thomas, did not believe. He had not been present

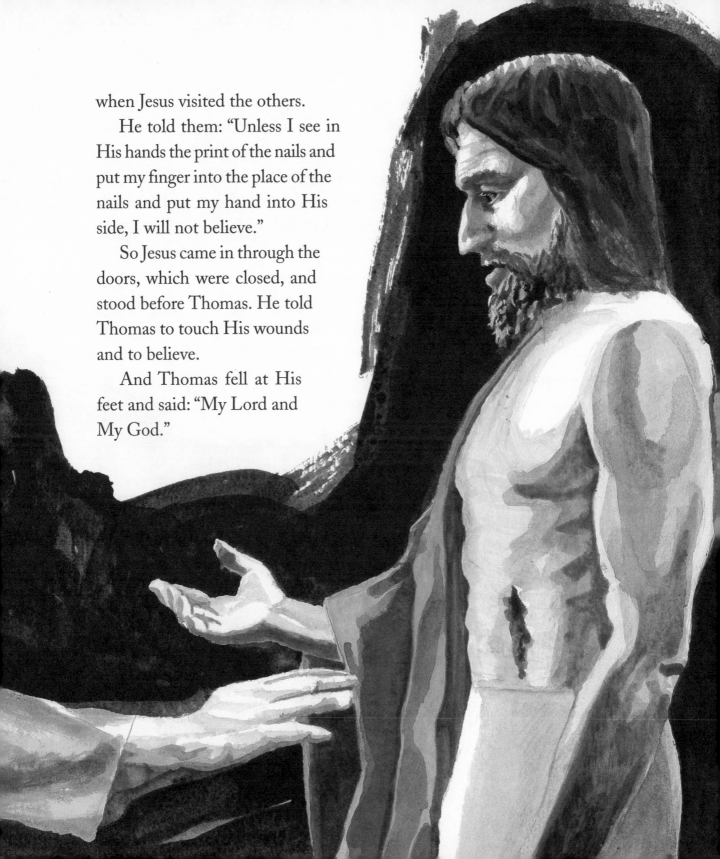

when Jesus visited the others.

He told them: "Unless I see in His hands the print of the nails and put my finger into the place of the nails and put my hand into His side, I will not believe."

So Jesus came in through the doors, which were closed, and stood before Thomas. He told Thomas to touch His wounds and to believe.

And Thomas fell at His feet and said: "My Lord and My God."

AFTER FORTY DAYS Jesus went back to Heaven.

But at the end of the world He will come again to judge the good and the bad. And those who have loved Him will live with Him forever.

It might be nice if Jesus had stayed on earth. Mothers could have taken their children to be blessed, and they could have seen the scars in His hands and feet and side which showed how He won the war against evil and sin.

But He said: "It is better for you that I go."

So, forty days after He rose from the dead, He went back to Heaven. And ten days later, on Pentecost, He sent His Spirit to us through the Apostles.

It is His Spirit which comes into the souls of all who love Him. Everyone might not have been able to visit Him if He had stayed on earth, but everyone can receive the gifts and blessings of His Spirit.

Our Father

Our Father, who art in heaven,
hallowed be Thy Name:
Thy kingdom come;
Thy will be done on earth as it is in heaven.
Give us this day our daily bread:
and forgive us our trespasses,
as we forgive those who trespass against us.
And lead us not into temptation.
But deliver us from evil.
Amen.

Hail Mary

Hail Mary, full of grace,
the Lord is with thee:
blessed art thou amongst women,
and blessed is the fruit of thy womb,
Jesus.

Holy Mary! Mother of God,
pray for us sinners,
now, and at the hour of our death.
Amen.